DISCARDED

HOLIDAY ORIGAMI

Easter

Origami

by Ruth Owen

press™

New York

Published in 2013 by The Rosen Publishing Group, Inc.
29 East 21st Street, New York, NY 10010

Produced for Rosen by Ruby Tuesday Books Ltd
Editor for Ruby Tuesday Books Ltd: Mark J. Sachner
US Editor: Sara Antill
Designer: Emma Randall

Photo Credits:
Cover, 1, 3, 5, 7, 8, 9 (top right), 12, 13 (top right), 16, 19, 20, 21 (top right), 24, 25 (top right), 28 © Shutterstock.
Origami models © Ruby Tuesday Books Ltd.

Library of Congress Cataloging-in-Publication Data

Owen, Ruth, 1967–
 Easter origami / by Ruth Owen.
     p. cm. — (Holiday origami)
 Includes index.
  ISBN 978-1-4488-7861-1 (library binding) — ISBN 978-1-4488-7920-5 (pbk.) — ISBN 978-1-4488-7926-7 (6-pack)
 1. Origami—Juvenile literature. 2. Easter decorations—Juvenile literature. I. Title.
 TT870.O947 2013
 736'.982—dc23

                                    2012009640

Manufactured in the United States of America

CPSIA Compliance Information: Batch # B4S12PK: For Further Information contact Rosen Publishing, New York, New York at 1-800-237-9932

Contents

Origami in Action

People have been making paper **sculptures** for hundreds of years. This Easter you can use the ancient art form of **origami** to create some fantastic paper Easter chicks, bunnies, and baskets.

Japan is one place where origami has been a popular pastime for centuries. Origami even gets its name from the Japanese words "ori," which means "folding," and "kami," which means "paper."

By just folding and creasing a single sheet of paper, origami model makers are able to make an animal, a vehicle, or even a beautiful flower. A three-dimensional origami model might involve dozens of tricky moves, while a simple, two-dimensional model might be created in less than five simple folds.

So, take a square of colorful paper, follow the step-by-step instructions in this book, and get folding some fantastic Easter origami!

4

Get Folding!

Before you get started on your Easter origami models, here are some tips.

Tip 1
Read all the instructions carefully and look at the pictures. Make sure you understand what's required before you begin a fold. Don't rush, but be patient. Work slowly and carefully.

Tip 2
Folding a piece of paper sounds easy, but it can be tricky to get neat, accurate folds. The more you practice, the easier it becomes.

Tip 3
If an instruction says "crease," make the crease as flat as possible. The flatter the creases, the better the model. You can make a sharp crease by running a plastic ruler along the edge of the paper.

Tip 4
Sometimes, at first, your models may look a little crumpled. Don't give up! The more models you make, the better you will get at folding and creasing.

When it comes to origami, practice makes perfect!

Check out these paper
rabbits and flowers made by an
experienced origami model maker.
In this book, you get the chance
to make tulips and an Easter bunny.
Keep practicing and soon you could
be making complicated models
like these!

One of the most popular origami models made in Japan is a bird called a crane. Most origami cranes will fit in a person's hand, but they don't have to be small.

In 1998, 200 people in the Japanese city of Odate made a giant origami crane with a wingspan of 207 feet (63 m)!

Happy Easter Egg!

Easter is the holiday on which Christians celebrate the **resurrection** of Jesus after his **crucifixion**. Easter is also a time for giving candy Easter eggs, bunnies, and chicks in celebration of the coming of spring, the season of birth and rebirth in nature.

A big part of many people's Easter fun, the Easter egg hunt, gives children a chance to add eggs, jelly beans, and other treats to their Easter baskets. Here is a simple origami project that will give you a chance to wish your family and friends a Happy Easter with beautiful Easter egg greeting cards.

To make Easter egg greetings cards, you will need:

Origami paper or scraps
of colored paper

Construction paper
or thin cardboard

Glue

(Origami paper is sometimes colored on both sides or white on one side.)

STEP 1:
To make an origami Easter egg, place a sheet of paper colored side down. Fold along the dotted line, and crease.

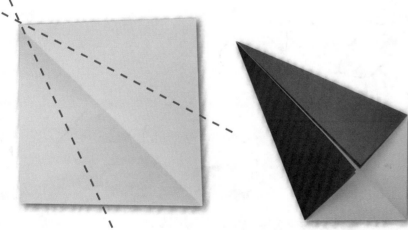

STEP 2:
Fold two sides into the center, and crease.

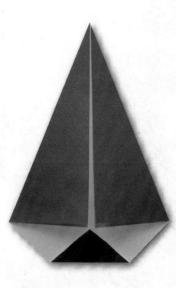

STEP 3:
Fold up the bottom point, and crease.

STEP 4:
Fold down the top point along the dotted line, and crease.

STEP 5:
Fold in the two sides along the dotted lines, and crease.

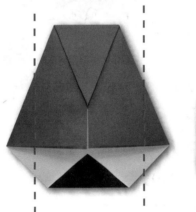

STEP 6:
Now fold down the two top corners to round off the top of your Easter egg.

STEP 7:
Turn the model over and your Easter egg is complete!

STEP 8:

Make Easter eggs in different colors or use scraps of colorful wrapping paper to make decorative patterned eggs.

STEP 9:

Fold a piece of construction paper in half and glue an egg to the front. Make sure you only put small dots of glue in three or four places so the egg looks 3D against the background. Write an Easter greeting.

Happy Easter!

Origami Easter Chick

From the deeply religious belief in the resurrection of Jesus to the awakening of nature after a long winter's sleep, the themes of birth and rebirth make Easter and spring go hand in hand. Farmers breed chickens to lay eggs year round. But spring is the season when the weather is warm enough for wild birds to have their young. So eggs and chicks have become two of the most beloved **symbols** of Easter.

This next wonderful origami creation is a yellow chick bursting from its egg. You can use it to decorate an Easter basket or glue it to the front of an Easter card!

To make an Easter chick, you will need:

Origami paper that is yellow on one side and white on the other

Black marker

(Origami paper is sometimes colored on both sides or white on one side.)

STEP 1:
Place the paper colored side down, fold in half diagonally, and crease. Then fold in half again.

STEP 2:
Turn the paper so the longest side is at the bottom. Fold the top flap of the paper back on itself, and crease.

STEP 3:
Now open out the top pocket of paper on the right side. Gently squash the pocket and fold it back down to form a square.

STEP 4:
Turn the model over. Now fold in the right side along the dotted line, and crease. Open out the top pocket of paper and then gently squash and fold it back down to form a square.

STEP 5:

Turn the model so that the open points are at the top. Fold both sides and the bottom into the center, and crease. Then unfold.

STEP 6:

Now pull open the top layer of paper. Then gently squash it back down to form a diamond shape, and crease.

STEP 7:

Fold up the bottom point of the diamond so it lays flat against the model.

STEP 8:

Turn the model over. Fold down the top layer of paper, and crease. Your model should look like this.

STEP 9:

Now fold down the two points at the top of the model to make the chick's wings, and crease.

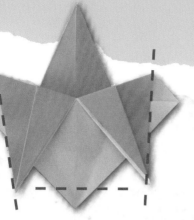

STEP 10:
Fold the three points behind the model, along the dotted lines, and crease.

STEP 11:
Fold down the top point to make the chick's head.

STEP 12:
Finally make two small folds at the pointed end of the chick's head to create its beak. Fold back the corners of its head to round off the shape. Draw on eyes, and your Easter chick is complete!

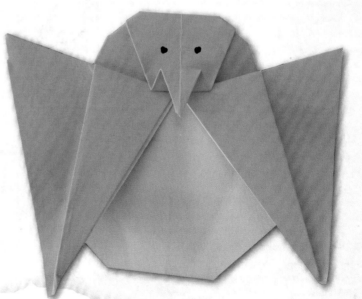

Easter Egg Display Stand

For centuries, eggs have been a sign of life and rebirth in spring. The tradition of coloring eggs to make them into Easter eggs also goes back for centuries. Early Christians stained eggs red in memory of the blood that Jesus shed during his crucifixion. In Poland and other nations in Eastern Europe, decorating eggs with beautiful designs became part of that tradition as Easter eggs were exchanged as gifts.

When eggs are dyed or decorated, they add color and art to brighten up an Easter celebration. This egg stand is a perfect way to display a brightly colored Easter egg when you've finished decorating it!

To make Easter egg display stands, you will need:

Origami paper in your favorite colors

(Origami paper is sometimes colored on both sides or white on one side.)

STEP 1:
Place the paper white side down, fold and crease along the dotted lines. Then fold the paper in half.

STEP 2:
Fold both sides of the model into the center, and crease.

STEP 3:
Fold down the two top corners, and crease. Then unfold.

STEP 4:
Open out the paper on both sides and gently squash flat. The triangular folds you made in step 3 will help the paper lie flat.

STEP 5:

Turn the model over, fold in the two sides, and crease.

STEP 6:

Now fold up the two bottom corners of the top layer of paper so they meet in the center, and crease well.

STEP 7:

Now fold up the point you've just made at the bottom of the model, flatten, and crease well.

STEP 8:
Turn the model over. Fold up the two bottom corners, and crease.

STEP 9:
Fold up the bottom point, and crease well.

STEP 10:
Finally, gently open out the pocket at the bottom of the model. Then squash down the white top part so the model becomes 3D and is ready to display an egg.

Easter Bunny

The tradition of the Easter Bunny bringing eggs and other gifts to children on Easter morning is an old one.

Odd as the connection between eggs and rabbits might seem, it comes from both of them being associated with bringing new life into the world. Eggs produce baby birds, and rabbits produce lots and lots of babies at once in large **litters**.

Here is a great origami design for a cute bunny that you can make this Easter.

To make an Easter bunny, you will need:

Colored pencils

Peel and stick
goggly eyes

Origami paper in your
favorite colors

(Origami paper is sometimes colored on both sides or white on one side.)

STEP 1:
Place the paper colored side down, fold in half diagonally, and crease. Then fold in half again.

STEP 2:
Turn the paper so the longest side is at the bottom, fold the top flap of the paper back on itself, and crease.

STEP 3:
Now open out the top pocket of paper on the right side. Gently squash the pocket back down to form a square.

STEP 4:
Turn the model over. Now fold in the right side along the dotted line, and crease. Open out the top pocket of paper and then gently squash and fold it back down to form a square.

STEP 5:
Turn the model so the open points are at the top. Fold down the top layer of paper to make the bunny's face, and crease.

STEP 6:
Now fold both sides of the top layer of paper behind the model, along the dotted lines, and crease.

STEP 7:
Fold the bottom point of the bunny's face behind, and crease.

STEP 8:
Turn the model over. Fold both sides and the bottom into the center, and crease. Then unfold. Fold up the bottom point again, so it meets the last fold you made, and crease.

A

STEP 9:

Now take hold of the top layer of paper at point A. Pull the paper down to open up the model. Then gently fold and squash the paper back in to form a diamond shape.

A

STEP 10:

Turn the model over and your bunny should look like this.

STEP 11:

Fold the sides of the body under to make it more 3D. Fold up the bottom point, and fold one of the bunny's ears down. Stick on goggly eyes and draw a nose and mouth, and your Easter bunny is complete!

Fold under

Fold under

Mini Easter Baskets

Going on an Easter egg hunt, with basket in hand, is as much a part of the celebration of Easter as eggs, bunnies, and chicks!

This simple origami project gives you a chance to make mini baskets of your own. Write names on them as place cards at dinner, or glue them to the front of handmade greeting cards. Place some jelly beans inside them for a special, added treat!

To make mini Easter baskets, you will need:

Origami paper in your favorite colors

Scissors

(Origami paper is sometimes colored on both sides or white on one side.)

STEP 1:
Place the paper colored side down, fold in half diagonally, and crease.

STEP 2:
Fold down the top layer of paper, and crease. Then unfold again.

STEP 3:
Now fold in the right side of the model, and crease.

STEP 4:
Now fold in the left side of the model, flatten, and crease.

STEP 5:
Fold the model in half, and crease.

STEP 6:
Now cut along the dotted line.

STEP 7:

Open up the model. Fold down one of the flaps that you've just cut, and crease.

STEP 8:

Turn the model over, fold down the other flap, and crease.

STEP 9:

The basket is complete!

Origami Tulips

Brightly colored daffodils and tulips are among the first flowers to blossom into life in spring. These flowers are colorful signs that winter is over and a new season has begun! Along with eggs, chicks, and bunnies, spring flowers in full bloom are also a reminder of the rebirth of life around Easter time.

Spring flowers make a wonderful Easter gift, and the best thing about these colorful origami tulips is that they will still be around long after Easter is over!

To make a tulip, you will need:

One sheet of origami paper for the flower and a green sheet for the leaf and stem

(Origami paper is sometimes colored on both sides or white on one side.)

STEP 1:
Place the paper colored side down, fold in half diagonally, and crease.

STEP 2:
Now fold the right side of the paper in along the dotted line, and crease.

STEP 3:

Now fold in the left side, and crease.

STEP 4:

Fold down the point at the top of the model to reveal the reverse of the paper, and crease.

STEP 5:

Fold the bottom point behind the model, crease, then unfold again. Now open up the model and use the fold you've just made to tuck in the bottom of the tulip flower to make a pocket.

STEP 6:

Close up the model again, and you will have a slot, or pocket, in the base of the tulip flower. You can use a little glue or tape if you wish to keep the flower's petals together.

Pocket

STEP 7:

To make the stem and leaf, place a sheet of green paper colored side down. Fold in half diagonally. Then open back up and fold in two sides so they meet in the center, and crease.

STEP 8:

Now fold the model in half along the center, and crease.

Top of stem

Leaf

STEP 9:

Fold up the bottom of the model to make the leaf, and crease. Fold the top point of the stem behind the model, and crease.

STEP 10:

Slide the top of the stem into the pocket at the base of the flower. Your tulip is complete!

Glossary

crucifixion (kroo-suh-FIK-shun) Putting someone to death by nailing or binding that person by the hands and feet to a cross.

litter (LIH-ter) A group of baby animals all born to the same mother at the same time.

origami (or-uh-GAH-mee) The art of folding paper into decorative shapes or objects.

resurrection (reh-zuh-REK-shun) Returning to life from death.

sculptures (SKULP-cherz) Works of art that have a shape to them, such as statues or carved objects, and may be made of wood, stone, metal, plaster, or even paper.

symbol (SIM-bul) Something that stands for or represents another thing, such as an important event or person.

Index

Websites